LO AND BEHOLD ...
DAILY WISDOM FROM THE LORD

CHRISTOPHER FERGUSON

Published by:
R. H. Publishing
3411 Preston Rd. Ste. C-13-146
Frisco, TX. 75034

Copyright © 2019, Christopher Ferguson

ISBN# 978-1-945693-31-1

All rights reserved under International Copyright Law. Written permission must be secured from the publisher/author to use or reproduce any part of this book.

TABLE OF CONTENTS

INTRODUCTION..9
VERILY I SAITH 11
KING OF KINGS AND LORD OF LORDS.......................12
PRIDE..13
YE ART A VESSEL..14
GENUINE REPENTANCE......................................15
THE WORD OF THE LORD....................................16
SHELTERED IN THE STORM.................................17
THE DEVIL LIES..18
SALVATION IS OUR KEY.....................................19
BE STILL..20
SEASONS...21
BEING ABOVE...22
THY FEET...23
SIN IS LIKE SALT...24
LIVE FOR CHRIST..25
STRAIN=GAIN...26
HEART ISSUES..27
GOD IS EVERYTHING... 28
THE FALSE LEADER...29

BEING WATCHFUL.	30
VICTORY IN DEATH	31
NOT I, BUT HIM	32
FOOLS	33
A RELATIONAL GOD	34
MY CHOICE	35
DESTRUCTION	36
DESIRES	37
GLORIFY THE LORD	38
RECEIVE COUNCIL	39
LASTING JOURNEY	40
FOOLISH TALK	41
GOD'S WORD	42
SPEAK	43
DIFFICULT TRIALS	44
DO NOT COMPARE	45
BEING PERFECT	46
OFFENSE	47
STONES	48
THE RIVER FLOWS	49
NO PAST=BRIGHT FUTURE	50
BE AWARE	51
LET HIM LEAD	52

DECEIVED	53
LIES	54
GOD'S GRACE	55
THE SCRIPTURES SPEAK	56
ACCEPT THE TRUTH	57
ONENESS IN CHRIST	58
TRUE HUNGER	59
PROVEN TRUTH	60
THE WORD	61
BEWARE	62
UNBROKEN	63
HIS HOLY UNION	64
REBUKE	65
MY LIFE IS CHRIST	66
LIFE	67
INTIMACY	68
UNQUENCHABLE THIRST	69
FREEING TRUTH	70
PRACTICE TO IDENTIFY	71
AN INTENTIONAL GOD	72
ETERNITY	73
MY TESTIMONY	74
REVELATIONS	75

WHAT DO YOU BELIEVE?	76
DO YOU FOLLOW?	77
DO YOU REMAIN DISOBEDIENT	78
ARE YOUR EYES OPEN?	79
ARE YOU LISTENING?	80
FEED ME	81
TASTE AND SEE	82
ENEMIES	83
IDENTITY IN CHRIST	84
FEAR NOT!	85
GLORY	86
PERFECT LOVE	87
THE LAW	88
IDENTITY ISSUE	89
LOVE	90
A HOLY THIRST	91
ATHEISM	92
OBEDIENCE	93
THE IRONY	94
CHRIST WITHIN	95
CHRIST'S PROMISE	96
MEDITATION	97
HONOR	98

HIS LOVE	99
SELF-DESTRUCTION	100
ENDLESS GLORY	101
LOVE SOOTHES	102
WOUNDS	103
I LOVE YOU	104
BLESSED CONVICTION	105
THE CUP	106
NOW I SEE	107
BEAUTIFUL CHRIST	108
PRESENTATION	109
EVIDENCE	110
LOVES PURPOSE	111
A DELIGHT	112
LED BY THE SPIRIT	113
TRUE ANSWERS	114
WHAT TRUTH?	115

INTRODUCTION

In this book, I do not desire to persuade my readers with catchy lines and impressive speech like doctrine, but to reveal my true motive, which is to interact with my readers in such a way that is truly intimate and raw in its delivery.

I am a man who believes in a personal relationship with the Holy Spirit. Therefore, my stance is emotionally captivated and orchestrated by the love of God and His words in me and through me.

My interactions with God have enabled me to pursue His righteousness in spirit and in truth. As you read, you will be captured by the level of intimacy, the Lord wants to have with all of His people.

Warning—this book is not to be read and discerned with your own understanding. It must only be read and treated with exegesis as the Holy Spirit shows you what He meant by the words you are about to read.

Hold on to your pen and paper ... throw them in the trash ... as this book shall teach you only about the most important gift in all spirituality ... Love is the only way and truth.

VERILY I SAITH

Verily I saith unto thee,

"Before ye lead,

ye must follow …

therein be Christ."

KING OF KINGS AND LORD OF LORDS

Kneel I shall to the King of Kings and Lord of Lords.

His sword is mine;

Mine, I saith mine,

to slay the perverse monstrosities that oppose Him.

PRIDE

It

is

the

very

thing

that leads to mankind's self-destruction.

YE ART A VESSEL

Thus, Ye art a vessel.

Thereon, be the handle—and not the hand.

Be carried—not the carrier.

The Lord Jesus Christ is thy hand and carrier

Who shatters not thy vessel.

GENUINE REPENTANCE

A genuine repentance discerns lies
and
demonstrates the Truth.

THE WORD OF THE LORD

The Word of the Lord must not be discerned by man.

But by the Holy Spirit.

Which is God.

SHELTERED IN THE STORM

The storm never dies.

He who prays and demonstrates thy Heavenly Father's ways shall be sheltered in the midst of it.

THE DEVIL LIES

The devil is a liar.

He offers piss and claims it to be wine.

SALVATION IS OUR KEY

In this life we all hold dearly our salvation.

It is a key that our signature is engraved on.

I beseech ye, "Why surrender thy key to the thief that hath not to enter into the Kingdom of Heaven when ye doth?"

BE STILL

Be still,

until thy Heavenly Father's will

hath been fulfilled.

SEASONS

The season hath come to pass.

Henceforth, it is of the past.

BEING ABOVE

He, who puts himself above others,

puts others above himself.

Thus, foolish he is to think less of himself.

THY FEET

Thy feet hast been where problems favor the deceit.

Thus, thy feet shall verily be where blessings favor the priest.

SIN IS LIKE SALT

Lo and behold …

sin is like salt.

It shall never quench thy thirst.

LIVE FOR CHRIST

Lo and behold ...

Live for Christ.

And not for thy own opinions and preferences.

STRAIN = GAIN

In this pain, thou shall receive blessings in Jesus name.

Thus, pay no attention to the strains of life,

but the gain of life.

HEART ISSUES

If pride is in your heart,
then Insecurity is in your soul.

GOD IS EVERYTHING

My God, my King, my everything.

I prithee,

Give me nary riches,

nor poorness that sores the heart of men.

THE FALSE LEADER

The Anti-Christ is the leader of all religions and cults.

BEING WATCHFUL

Lo and behold … be watchful.

In the realm of the spirit, thou shall win many battles,

but the war is never over

until Thy Kingdom comes.

VICTORY IN DEATH

Lo and behold ...

Many shall face death to be resurrected.

NOT I—BUT HIM

I define not myself.

I am rather defined by the Lord Jesus Christ.

Thus, I am led to believe.

FOOLS

Fools make enemies among friends.

A RELATIONAL GOD

Lo and behold ...

The Lord Jesus Christ is a God of Relationship.

MY CHOICE

Lo and behold ...

I choose to die on my feet for the Prince of Peace.

Than to die on my knees to the devil's final deceit.

DESTRUCTION

Lo and behold ...

The works of the enemy are to destroy its host

and other people who matter the most.

DESIRES

Remove the desires to sin,

by replacing them with the desires to prevail within.

GLORIFY THE LORD

Lo and behold …

glorify the Lord Jesus Christ

in all things that thou doeth.

RECEIVE COUNSEL

Lo and behold ...

Blessed is he who receives the counsel of the kind in heart, and turneth away from the evil that scars the heart.

LASTING JOURNEY

Lo and behold ...

Alone, but never alone.

A journey well written and told.

To inherit the Kingdom of Heaven—my home.

I shall, in time, kneel before the throne.

FOOLISH TALK

Lo and behold ...

Fools cut their own tongue out

with their unrighteous words.

GOD'S WORD

He that giveth the Word of God,

giveth food to the poor.

Thus, let all be filled with truth and love.

SPEAK

Speak my Heavenly Father.

Thy words art priceless to save souls,

and to make miracles unfold.

DIFFICULT TRIALS

Lo and behold ...

In all difficult trials quiet thy mind,

and listen to thy heart.

DO NOT COMPARE

To all women I say, "Never compare yourself to others."

No woman looks better than you.

Thus, you are the most beautiful you.

That is the unchangeable truth.

BEING PERFECT

Lo and behold …

Be perfect as thy identity in Christ is perfect.

OFFENSE

Lo and behold ...

Fools take offense

whenever the wisdom of Christ

corrects their blunders.

STONES

Lo and behold ...

I walk on the stones that thy Heavenly Father

hast placed for me to roam.

THE RIVER FLOWS

Lo and behold ...

He who accepts his identity in Christ

hath made himself perfect.

Thus, he is like a river that floweth in one direction

and no other.

NO PAST = BRIGHT FUTURE

Lo and behold …

Dost not let the cursed past

take form of thy blessed future.

Thereon, whatever is pure,

holdeth no impurity.

BE AWARE

Lo and behold ...

The eyes may see,

and the ears may hear.

The Lies cannot see truth,

and the dead cannot hear and be aware.

LET HIM LEAD

Lo and behold ...

To defeat sin is to be led within

by He Who always wins.

DECEIVED

Lo and behold ...

The faithless hath no true answer,

yet they claim a wrongful truth.

LIES

Lo and behold ...

Lies claim Truth exists not,

but believe in the words—Truth and Lies.

GOD'S GRACE

Lo and behold ...

My judgment hast torn and sored,

but Thy Heavenly Father's judgment hast nurtured and cured.

Thus, accept God's grace that giveth thee away

out of thy pain.

THE SCRIPTURES SPEAK

Lo and behold ...

The Scriptures speak.

Thus, He need neither tongue nor teeth,

but an obedient sheet.

ACCEPT THE TRUTH

I am no respecter of men and their philosophy.

I only desire God and His commands.

Therefore, I accept the truth, and I am the truth.

ONENESS IN CHRIST

I hast found no one that can relate to my oneness in Christ. Only because they art not willing enough.

TRUE HUNGER

Do not mistake willingness for hunger!

Hunger is he who is made righteous.

Willingness is he who is made whole.

PROVEN TRUTH

Everything that I hast heard from the Father proves true.

To a degree of certainty.

THE WORD

I confess!

That Scriptures art no longer relevant.

Only!

The Word of God.

BEWARE

Lies linger where hearts seem true.

UNBROKEN

They have broken my arms and legs,

but verily they cannot break my heart.

HIS HOLY UNION

I would marry any woman

as long as my Heavenly Father

desires the union

to be His own.

REBUKE

I welcome a double-minded Christian with a healthy rebuke.

MY LIFE IS CHRIST

My obedience is not to a Bible,

nor is my alliance to the father of satanic disciples.

Thus, my title is my life, and my life is Christ.

LIFE

Christ's death brought me closer to life.

Life taught me how to die daily.

In the end, eternal life shall be my reward.

Thus, be the living sacrifice God Almighty intended for all men to be and not an unworthy sacrifice.

INTIMACY

The Word of God

without intimacy

is death.

UNQUENCHABLE THIRST

I foolishly drink water

that I may quench

my unquenchable thirst for the Lord.

FREEING TRUTH

Brothers and sisters, I must speak the truth.

I am the truth, and the truth hath set me free.

Though I am tempted,

I hast no appetite for sin.

Indeed, sin is savory,

but my palette is already salted with fire.

PRACTICE TO IDENTIFY

I am sad to say,
some of God's people art stuck in their ways,
because they do not practice
to identify the Word of God.

AN INTENTIONAL GOD

Many shall say I am more than a man.

I am what God Intended man to be.

ETERNITY

Truly! I hast no time for the world.

Let the world Indulge in itself.

I've only eternity for my one and only.

MY TESTIMONY

My Testimony

Lo! The intimacy grows.

Like a vineyard kept by the son of man.

REVELATIONS

I speak revelations, that art the validations of truth.

Thus, if my revelations art not found in ye.

Then ye art against me and the Father.

WHAT DO YOU BELIEVE?

If you say what you believe …

Why do you not believe what you say?

DO YOU FOLLOW?

If you do what is written in the scrolls and Bible …

Why do you not follow the Word of God in your heart?

DO YOU REMAIN DISOBEDIENT?

Why do you persist in being good in your own eyes,

but remain disobedient?

ARE YOUR EYES OPEN?

Why are your eyes open,

but you have kept them shut?

ARE YOU LISTENING?

Why have you presented your body as a living sacrifice, but you have not listened to Me and responded to My voice?

FEED ME

I starve forever more.

TASTE AND SEE

I taste the bitterness and sweetness of the Lord.

Truly it is an acquired taste.

ENEMIES

I do not hast more enemies.

I've only encountered new vessels that art occupied by evil.

IDENTITY IN CHRIST

My mother's requests on behalf of her son,

came forth into being as immense power.

Yet, she could not fathom my identity in Christ.

FEAR NOT!

I fear not!

These satanic forces.

Truly, I am ruthless with them that art truthless.

The Word of God is my favorite weapon!

I kid you not, when I say, "All demons that face my wrath, walketh in dry places—deaf, dumb and blind."

GLORY

Too much glory is never enough glory!

PERFECT LOVE

Sin did not conceive perfect love.

Thus, it cannot understand Him.

THE LAW

All things art lawful … and all things art not lawful. Thus, be advised and committed by the Enforcer of the law, as He is greater than the law itself.

IDENTITY ISSUE

In Christ ... the limits seek out the limitless.
Yet, the limits settle for the limited
because they hast not known that the limitless
hast proclaimed the limits limitless.

LOVE

Men envy the love in my heart,

but it is not my own.

As I am only a son to the Father above.

A HOLY THIRST

The holy unquenchable thirst lingers forever more.

ATHEISM

It is evident that with so much darkness

the fool would believe thither is no light.

OBEDIENCE

Even if Satan had a way,
my obedience for Christ triumphs over all.

THE IRONY

The irony of loving what I hate

and hating what I love

shall prevail and not hate.

CHRIST WITHIN

I commend the Christ within me

as great is His love

and long is His endurance.

CHRIST'S PROMISE

If life bestowed death

in exchange for eternal life,

then surely death is imminent

in order for life to be worth-while.

This is the promise of Christ!

MEDITATION

Brethren face thy reality.

It was for my own peace that I had great bitterness.

Thus, whatever is true and honorable ...

meditate upon it!

As the voice of the Lord shall never be silenced.

HONOR

Brethren fear not …

But fear the Lord

that thou shall be honored in His eyes.

Thus, the honor is greater than the fear of the enemy.

HIS LOVE

No pride is in His glory

as His glory surely restores me.

Thus, to God be the glory

as His love standeth before me.

SELF-DESTRUCTION

The prideful man shall gain a prideful plan.

The end of all pride is self-destruction.

ENDLESS GLORY

Endless glory waits before me.

The heavens shall tell my story of a child

Who gave His glory to the One and only.

LOVE SOOTHES

I hast taken my afflictions,

and made it sooth my body, mind and soul

by the power and poetry of love.

WOUNDS

My wounds and sores hast became painless afflictions and woundless conviction.

I LOVE YOU

I love her so much.

So much, I love her.

I can touch her soul and taste the words she spoke.

I love you, Jesus Christ.

BLESSED CONVICTION

Drench me with your tears.

Taste me on your lips.

Hold me in your arm my blessed conviction.

THE CUP

I feel Heaven.

Truly a cup of love quenches the thirst.

However, the cup can never be filled enough.

NOW I SEE

You who seek Me out.

Though you were blind …

now you see,

and you see Me.

BEAUTIFUL CHRIST

These sores and wounds shall make for beautiful scars.

Truly, beauty is in the eyes of the beholder …

Christ.

PRESENTATION

I want a lady who can take care of these

uninhabited wounds and fearless scars.

Dress me in a suit.

Present me as a living sacrifice before the Father.

EVIDENCE

I paste these words on your heart so deeply.

Holes say stretch forth your arms.

Look how you hast pierced me.

Look how you hast killed me with your sobering love.

LOVES PURPOSE

Love is not an emotion.

Love is willingness.

Therefore, love gives birth to emotions.

A DELIGHT

In person, I am quite a delight.

Though it is not my appearance,

but my absolute oneness in Christ.

LED BY THE SPIRIT

Lo and behold ...

A man can speak the words from a Bible

and teach from it,

but if he is not led by the Holy Spirit,

he can neither read nor teach truth,

but speak deceit through his teeth.

TRUE ANSWERS

Lo and behold …

The faithless hath no true answer;

Yet, they claim a wrongful truth.

WHAT TRUTH?

Lo and behold …

Lies claim that truth exists not,

but believe in the words truth and lies.

ABOUT THE AUTHOR

Christopher Ferguson was an honor student at the University of Technology, where he pursued a Bachelor of Education (B.Ed), specializing in Industrial Technology and major Construction Technology.

In 2018, he was generously given a Departmental Full-work Scholarship to attend Christ For The Nations Institute in Dallas, Texas. At CFNI he will complete his Bachelor's Degree in Practical Theology.

To reach Christopher, go to:

Email: christopherferguson1994@gmail.com

Instagram: fergusonchristopher_

Amazon: christopher ferguson www.amazon.com/gp/profile/amzn1.account.

AEHCNWBWJ5LJ6PQ4QSGVF4KAUCIQ

www.ingramcontent.com/pod-product-compliance
Lightning Source LLC
Chambersburg PA
CBHW060031180426
43196CB00044B/2374